TO

_____

FROM

_____

FIRST CUP
DEVOTIONS

FOR
WOMEN

FAMILY CHRISTIAN PRESS
Grand Rapids, MI 49530

The quoted ideas expressed in this book (but not scripture verses) are not, in all cases, exact quotations, as some have been edited for clarity and brevity. In all cases, the author has attempted to maintain the speaker's original intent. In some cases, quoted material for this book was obtained from secondary sources, primarily print media. While every effort was made to ensure the accuracy of these sources, the accuracy cannot be guaranteed. For additions, deletions, corrections or clarifications in future editions of this text, please write FAMILY CHRISTIAN PRESS.

Scripture quotations are taken from:

The Holy Bible, King James Version

The Holy Bible, New International Version (NIV) Copyright © 1973, 1978, 1984, by International Bible Society. Used by permission of Zondervan Publishing House. All rights reserved.

The Holy Bible, New King James Version (NKJV) Copyright © 1982 by Thomas Nelson, Inc. Used by permission.

The New American Standard Bible®, (NASB) Copyright © 1960, 1962, 1963, 1968, 1971, 1972, 1973, 1975, 1977, 1995 by The Lockman Foundation. Used by permission.

Holy Bible, New Living Translation, (NLT)copyright © 1996. Used by permission of Tyndale House Publishers, Inc., Wheaton, Illinois 60189. All rights reserved.

The Message (MSG)- This edition issued by contractual arrangement with NavPress, a division of The Navigators, U.S.A. Originally published by NavPress in English as THE MESSAGE: The Bible in Contemporary Language copyright 2002-2003 by Eugene Peterson. All rights reserved.

New Century Version®. (NCV) Copyright © 1987, 1988, 1991 by Word Publishing, a division of Thomas Nelson, Inc. All rights reserved. Used by permission.

The Holman Christian Standard Bible™ (HCSB) Copyright © 1999, 2000, 2001 by Holman Bible Publishers. Used by permission.

Cover Design by Kim Russell / Wahoo Designs
Page Layout by Bart Dawson

ISBN 1-58334-272-9

FIRST CUP
DEVOTIONS

FOR
WOMEN

TABLE OF CONTENTS

Introduction: First Things First   9

Day 1 It All Starts with God   11

Day 2 The Words You Speak Today   15

Day 3 A Day of Thanksgiving   19

Day 4 A Time for Obedience   23

Day 5 A Day Filled with Love   27

Day 6 Trusting God Day by Day   31

Day 7 The Power of Patience   35

Day 8 A Time for Generosity   39

Day 9 Forgiveness Today   43

Day 10 A Time for Renewal   47

Day 11 Sensing God's Presence Today   51

Day 12 Beyond Busyness   55

Day 13 The Right Kind of Example   59

Day 14 A Woman of Integrity   63

Day 15 The Attitude You Choose   67

Day 16 The Willingness to Help   71

Day 17 Sharing Your Testimony   75

Day 18 Experiencing the Joy   79

Day 19 Making Time for Silence   83

Day 20 The Power of Faith   87

Day 21 Accepting God's Spiritual Abundance   91

Day 22 Priorities That Are Pleasing to God   95

Day 23 A Day of Prayer   99

Day 24 Cheerfulness in the Here and Now   103

Day 25 Taking Time to Encourage Others   107

Day 26 When the Day Is Difficult   111

Day 27 Spiritual Growth Day by Day   115

Day 28 Wisdom for Today   119

Day 29 Today: God's Gift to You   123

Day 30 Accepting God's Love Today   127

Bible Verses to Consider   131

INTRODUCTION:
FIRST THINGS FIRST

How do you start your day? Do you awaken early enough to enjoy that first cup of hot coffee while studying your Bible and spending a few quiet moments with God? Or are you one of those women who sleep until the last possible minute, leaving no time to invest in matters of the heart and soul? Hopefully, you make a habit of spending precious moments each morning with your Creator. When you do, He will fill your heart, He will direct your thoughts, and He will guide your steps.

Daily life is woven together with the threads of habit, and no habit is more important to your spiritual growth than the discipline of daily prayer and devotion to God.

This book contains devotional readings that are intended to set the tone for the rest of your day. The text is divided into 30 chapters, one for each day of the month. Each chapter contains Bible verses, quotations, brief essays, and prayers, all of which can help you focus your thoughts on the countless blessings and opportunities that God has placed before you.

During the next 30 days, please try this experiment: Read one chapter each morning with your first cup of coffee. If you're already committed to a daily worship time, this book will enrich that experience. If you are not, the simple act of giving God a few minutes each morning will change the tone and direction of your life.

Your daily devotional time can be habit-forming, and should be. The first few minutes of each day are invaluable. Treat them that way, and offer them to God.

IT ALL STARTS WITH GOD

YOU SHALL HAVE NO OTHER GODS BEFORE ME.

EXODUS 20:3 NKJV

Does God come first in your life *and* your day? Hopefully so. When Jesus was tempted by Satan, the Master's response was unambiguous. Jesus chose to worship the Lord and "serve Him only" (Matthew 4:10 HCSB). We, as believers in Christ, must follow in His footsteps by placing God first.

When we mistakenly place God in a position of secondary importance, we do ourselves great harm. When we allow the obligations of everyday life to come between us and our Creator, we suffer. But, when we imitate Jesus and place the Lord in His rightful place—at the center of our lives—then we claim spiritual treasures that will endure forever.

When we begin each day with heads bowed and hearts lifted, we remind ourselves of God's love, His protection, and His commandments. And if we are wise, we align our priorities for the coming day with the teachings and commandments that God has given us through His Holy Word.

Are you in the habit of talking to your Creator each morning? If so, you're to be congratulated. There's no better way to start your day than with a steaming cup of coffee and a heartfelt conversation with God.

Our ultimate aim in life is not to be healthy,
wealthy, prosperous, or problem free.
Our ultimate aim in life is to bring glory to God.

ANNE GRAHAM LOTZ

Jesus Christ is the first and last, author and finisher,
beginning and end, alpha and omega,
and by Him all other things hold together.
He must be first or nothing. God never comes next!

VANCE HAVNER

Give God what's right—not what's left!

ANONYMOUS

I lived with Indians who made pots out of clay
which they used for cooking. Nobody was interested
in the pot. Everybody was interested in what
was inside. The same clay taken out of the same
riverbed, always made in the same design,
nothing special about it. Well, I'm a clay pot,
and let me not forget it. But, the excellency of
the power is of God and not us.

ELISABETH ELLIOT

MORE FROM GOD'S WORD

He that loveth not, knoweth not God; for God is love.

1 JOHN 4:8 KJV

This is the message which we have heard from Him and declare to you, that God is light and in Him is no darkness at all.

1 JOHN 1:5 NKJV

TODAY, I WILL THINK ABOUT . . .

Ways that I can glorify God by placing Him first in my life.

A PRAYER TO START MY DAY

Dear Lord, Your love is eternal and Your laws are everlasting. When I obey Your commandments, I am blessed. Today, I invite You to reign over every corner of my heart. I will have faith in You; I will sense Your presence; I will accept Your love; I will trust Your will; and I will praise You for the Savior of my life: Your Son Jesus. **Amen

THE WORDS YOU SPEAK TODAY

CARELESS WORDS STAB LIKE A SWORD,

BUT WISE WORDS BRING HEALING.

PROVERBS 12:18 NCV

As you think about the day ahead, think about the quality and tone of the words you intend to speak. Hopefully, you understand that your words have great power . . . because they most certainly do. If your words are encouraging, you can lift others up; if your words are hurtful, you can hold others back.

The Bible makes it clear that "Careless words stab like a sword." So, if you hope to solve problems instead of starting them, you must measure your words carefully. But sometimes, you'll be tempted to speak first and think second (with decidedly mixed results).

When you're frustrated or tired, you may say things that would be better left unspoken. Whenever you lash out in anger, you forgo the wonderful opportunity to consider your thoughts before you give voice to them. When you speak impulsively, you may, quite unintentionally, injure others.

A far better strategy, of course, is to do the more difficult thing: to think first and to speak next. When you do so, you give yourself ample time to compose your thoughts and to consult your Creator (but not necessarily in that order!)

Do you seek to be the kind of woman who is a continuing source of encouragement to others? Do you want to be a beacon of hope to your friends and family? And, do you seek to be a worthy ambassador for Christ? If so, you must speak words that are worthy of your Savior. So avoid angry outbursts. Refrain from impulsive outpourings. Terminate tantrums. Instead, speak words of encouragement and hope to a world that desperately needs both.

* * * * * * *

We will always experience regret when we live for the moment and do not weigh our words and deeds before we give them life.

LISA BEVERE

When you talk, choose the very same words that you would use if Jesus were looking over your shoulder. Because He is.

MARIE T. FREEMAN

MORE FROM GOD'S WORD

And whatsoever ye do in word or deed,
do all in the name of the Lord Jesus,
giving thanks to God and the Father by him.

COLOSSIANS 3:17 KJV

Watch the way you talk.
Let nothing foul or dirty come out of your mouth.
Say only what helps, each word a gift.

EPHESIANS 4:29 MSG

TODAY, I WILL THINK ABOUT . . .

The importance of measuring my words carefully,
especially when I'm angry.

A PRAYER TO START MY DAY

Dear Lord, You have commanded me to choose
my words carefully so that I might be a source of
encouragement and hope to all whom I meet. Keep
me mindful, Lord, that I have influence on many
people. Let the words that I speak today be worthy
of the One who has saved me forever. **Amen

A DAY OF THANKSGIVING

AND LET THE PEACE OF GOD RULE
IN YOUR HEARTS, TO WHICH ALSO
YOU WERE CALLED IN ONE BODY;
AND BE THANKFUL.

COLOSSIANS 3:15 NKJV

If you're like most females on the planet, you're a very busy woman. Your life is probably hectic, demanding, and complicated. When the demands of life leave you rushing from place to place with scarcely a moment to spare, you may fail to pause and thank your Creator for the blessings He has bestowed upon you. Big mistake.

No matter how busy you are, you should never be too busy to thank God for His gifts. Your task, as a radical believer in a living Christ, is to praise God many times each day. Then, with gratitude in your heart, you can face your daily duties with the perspective and power that only He can provide.

As you plan for the day ahead, make plans to thank God for all His blessings. You owe your Heavenly Father everything, including your eternal praise . . . starting right now.

God has promised that if we harvest well
with the tools of thanksgiving, there will be seeds
for planting in the spring.

GLORIA GAITHER

Thanksgiving or complaining—these words express
two contrastive attitudes of the souls of
God's children in regard to His dealings with them.
The soul that gives thanks can find comfort in
everything; the soul that complains can find
comfort in nothing.

HANNAH WHITALL SMITH

The act of thanksgiving is a demonstration of
the fact that you are going to trust and believe God.

KAY ARTHUR

The best way to show my gratitude to God is
to accept everything, even my problems, with joy.

MOTHER TERESA

God is worthy of our praise and is pleased
when we come before Him with thanksgiving.

SHIRLEY DOBSON

MORE FROM GOD'S WORD

Give thanks in all circumstances;
for this is God's will for you in Christ Jesus.

1 THESSALONIANS 5:18 NIV

Thanks be to God for His indescribable gift!

2 CORINTHIANS 9:15 NKJV

TODAY, I WILL THINK ABOUT . . .

The urgent need to thank God for His gifts.

A PRAYER TO START MY DAY

Lord, let me be a thankful Christian.
Your blessings are priceless and eternal.
I praise You, Lord, for Your gifts and, most of all,
for Your Son. Your love endures forever.
I will offer You my heartfelt thanksgiving
this day and throughout all eternity. **Amen

A TIME FOR OBEDIENCE

FOR IT IS NOT MERELY KNOWING
THE LAW THAT BRINGS GOD'S APPROVAL.
THOSE WHO OBEY THE LAW WILL BE
DECLARED RIGHT IN GOD'S SIGHT.

ROMANS 2:13 NLT

How can we demonstrate our love for God? By accepting His Son as our personal Savior and by placing Christ squarely at the center of our lives and our hearts. Jesus said that if we are to love Him, we must obey His commandments (John 14:15). Thus, our obedience to the Master is an expression of our love for Him.

In Ephesians 2:10 we read, "For we are His workmanship, created in Christ Jesus for good works" (NKJV). These words are instructive: We are not saved by good works, but for good works. Good works are not the root, but rather the fruit of our salvation.

Today, let the fruits of your stewardship be a clear demonstration of your love for Christ. When you do, your good heart will bring forth many good things for yourself and for God. Christ has given you spiritual abundance and eternal life. You, in turn, owe Him good treasure from a single obedient heart: yours.

If you want to discover your spiritual gifts,
start obeying God. As you serve Him,
you will find that He has given you the gifts that
are necessary to follow through in obedience.

ANNE GRAHAM LOTZ

Our obedience does not make God any bigger or
better than He already is. Anything God commands
of us is so that our joy may be full—the joy of seeing
His glory revealed to us and in us!

BETH MOORE

God does not want the forced obedience of slaves.
Instead, He covets the voluntary love and obedience
of children who love Him for Himself.

CATHERINE MARSHALL

Obedience is the key of knowledge.

CHRISTINA ROSSETTI

Perfect obedience would be perfect happiness,
if only we had perfect confidence
in the power we were obeying.

CORRIE TEN BOOM

MORE FROM GOD'S WORD

*Jesus answered, "If anyone loves Me,
he will keep My word. My Father will love him, and
We will come to him and make Our home with him."*

JOHN 14:23 HCSB

*When people do not accept divine guidance,
they run wild. But whoever obeys the law is happy.*

PROVERBS 29:18 NLT

TODAY, I WILL THINK ABOUT . . .

The importance of obedience and
the destructive nature of sin.

A PRAYER TO START MY DAY

Dear Lord, when I am tempted to disobey
Your commandments, correct my errors and guide
my path. Make me a faithful steward of my talents,
my opportunities, and my possessions so that Your
kingdom may be glorified, now and forever. **Amen

A DAY FILLED WITH LOVE

NOW THESE THREE REMAIN:

FAITH, HOPE, AND LOVE.

BUT THE GREATEST OF THESE IS LOVE.

1 CORINTHIANS 13:13 HCSB

As a woman, you know the profound love that you hold in your heart for your own family and friends. As a child of God, you can only imagine the infinite love that your Heavenly Father holds for you.

God made you in His own image and gave you salvation through the person of His Son Jesus Christ. And now, precisely because you are a wondrous creation treasured by God, a question presents itself: What will you do in response to the Creator's love? Will you ignore it or embrace it? Will you return it or neglect it? That decision, of course, is yours and yours alone.

When you embrace God's love, your life's purpose is forever changed. When you embrace God's love, you feel differently about yourself, your neighbors, your family, and your world. More importantly, you share God's message—and His love—with others.

Your Heavenly Father—a God of infinite love and mercy—is waiting to embrace you with open arms. Accept His love today and forever.

Accustom yourself continually to make many
acts of love, for they enkindle and melt the soul.

ST. TERESA OF AVILA

You can't really love other people well
unless you are at home in your own soul.
You will simply be too afraid.

PAULA RINEHART

Those who abandon ship the first time it enters
a storm miss the calm beyond. And the rougher
the storms weathered together,
the deeper and stronger real love grows.

RUTH BELL GRAHAM

The reason why God's servants love creatures
so much is that they see how much Christ loves
them, and it is one of the properties of love
to love what is loved by the person we love.

ST. CATHERINE OF SIENA

Love can't be pinned down by a definition,
and it certainly can't be proved, any more than
anything else important in life can be proved.

MADELEINE L'ENGLE

MORE FROM GOD'S WORD

Love does no harm to its neighbor.
Therefore love is the fulfillment of the law.
ROMANS 13:10 NIV

Many waters cannot quench love,
neither can the floods drown it.
SONG OF SOLOMON 8:7 KJV

TODAY, I WILL THINK ABOUT . . .

Creative ways that I can express love
to my family and friends.

A PRAYER TO START MY DAY

Dear Lord, Your love for me is infinite and eternal.
Let me acknowledge Your love, accept
Your love, and share Your love. Make me a woman
of compassion, understanding, and forgiveness.
And let the love that I feel in my heart
be expressed through kind words,
good deeds, and heartfelt prayers. **Amen

TRUSTING GOD DAY BY DAY

TRUST IN THE LORD WITH
ALL YOUR HEART, AND LEAN NOT
ON YOUR OWN UNDERSTANDING;
IN ALL YOUR WAYS ACKNOWLEDGE HIM,
AND HE SHALL DIRECT YOUR PATHS.

PROVERBS 3:5-6 NKJV

When our dreams come true and our plans prove successful, we find it easy to thank our Creator and easy to trust His divine providence. But in times of sorrow or hardship, we may find ourselves questioning God's plans for our lives.

On occasion, you will confront circumstances that trouble you to the very core of your soul. It is during these difficult days that you must find the wisdom and the courage to trust your Heavenly Father despite your circumstances.

Are you a woman who seeks God's blessings for yourself and your family? Then trust Him. Trust Him with your relationships. Trust Him with your priorities. Follow His commandments and pray for His guidance. Trust Your Heavenly Father day by day, moment by moment—in good times and in trying times. Then, wait patiently for God's revelations . . . and prepare yourself for the abundance and peace that will most certainly be yours when you do.

Faith is nothing more or less than
actively trusting God.

CATHERINE MARSHALL

The more we learn to receive and depend upon
His grace in deepening measure, the less anxious
we will be about what the future holds.

CYNTHIA HEALD

Make the least of all that goes and the most
of all that comes. Don't regret what is past.
Cherish what you have. Look forward to all
that is to come. And most important of all,
rely moment by moment on Jesus Christ.

GIGI GRAHAM TCHIVIDJIAN

It helps to resign as the controller of your fate.
All that energy we expend
to keep things running right
is not what keeps things running right.

ANNE LAMOTT

MORE FROM GOD'S WORD

He heeded their prayer,
because they put their trust in him.

1 CHRONICLES 5:20 NKJV

For we walk by faith, not by sight.

2 CORINTHIANS 5:7 NASB

TODAY, I WILL THINK ABOUT . . .

The need to trust God in *every* aspect of my life.

A PRAYER TO START MY DAY

Dear Lord, this morning I come to You with hope in my heart and praise on my lips. I place my trust in You, dear God, knowing that with You as my Protector, I have nothing to fear. I thank You, Father, for Your grace, for Your Love, and for Your Son. Let me follow in Christ's footsteps today and every day that I live. And then, when my work here is done, let me live with You forever. **Amen

THE POWER OF PATIENCE

GOD BLESSES THE PEOPLE
WHO PATIENTLY ENDURE TESTING.
AFTERWARD THEY WILL RECEIVE
THE CROWN OF LIFE THAT GOD
HAS PROMISED TO THOSE WHO LOVE HIM.

JAMES 1:12 NLT

Are you a woman in a hurry? If so, you may be in for a few disappointments. Why? Because life has a way of unfolding according to God's timetable, not yours. That's why life requires patience . . . and lots of it!

Lamentations 3:25-26 reminds us that, "The Lord is wonderfully good to those who wait for him and seek him. So it is good to wait quietly for salvation from the LORD" (NIV). But, for most of us, waiting quietly for God is difficult because we're in such a hurry for things to happen!

The next time you find your patience tested to the limit, slow down and trust God. Sometimes, we must wait patiently for Him, and that's as it should be. After all, think how patient God has been with us.

We must learn to wait.
There is grace supplied to the one who waits.

MRS. CHARLES E. COWMAN

Let me encourage you to continue to wait
with faith. God may not perform a miracle,
but He is trustworthy to touch you and make you
whole where there used to be a hole.

LISA WHELCHEL

How do you wait upon the Lord?
First you must learn to sit at His feet and
take time to listen to His words.

KAY ARTHUR

The times we find ourselves having to wait
on others may be the perfect opportunities
to train ourselves to wait on the Lord.

JONI EARECKSON TADA

God may say "Wait," but He never says, "Worry."

ANONYMOUS

MORE FROM GOD'S WORD

*The LORD is wonderfully good to those who
wait for him and seek him. So it is good to wait quietly
for salvation from the LORD.*

LAMENTATIONS 3:25-26 NLT

*Wait patiently on the LORD. Be brave and courageous.
Yes, wait patiently on the LORD.*

PSALM 27:14 NLT

TODAY, I WILL THINK ABOUT . . .

Becoming more patient with others,
with myself, and with God.

A PRAYER TO START MY DAY

Lord, make me a woman of patience. When I am
hurried, give me peace. When I am frustrated,
give me perspective. When I am angry, let me
turn my heart to You. Today, let me be a patient
Christian, dear Lord, as I trust in You and
in Your master plan for my life. **Amen

A TIME FOR GENEROSITY

EACH PERSON SHOULD DO AS HE HAS
DECIDED IN HIS HEART—
NOT OUT OF REGRET OR OUT OF NECESSITY,
FOR GOD LOVES A CHEERFUL GIVER.

2 CORINTHIANS 9:7 HCSB

As you begin your day consider this: the thread of generosity is woven—completely and inextricably—into the very fabric of Christ's teachings. As He sent His disciples out to heal the sick and spread God's message of salvation, Jesus offered this guiding principle: Freely you have received, freely give (Matthew 10:8 NIV). The principle still applies. If we are to be disciples of Christ, we must give freely of our time, our possessions, and our love.

Lisa Whelchel spoke for Christian women everywhere when she observed, "The Lord has abundantly blessed me all of my life. I'm not trying to pay Him back for all of His wonderful gifts; I just realize that He gave them to me to give away." All of us have been blessed, and all of us are called to share those blessings without reservation.

Today, make this pledge and keep it: Be a cheerful, generous, courageous giver. The world needs your help, and you need the spiritual rewards that will be yours when you share your possessions, your talents, and your time.

Giving from a grateful heart and expecting nothing
in return is a sweet offering to the One who owns
everything I have anyway. It's the very least
I can do. And as I give, I experience God's grace.

MARY HUNT

To show great love for God and our neighbor,
we need not do great things. It is how much love
we put in the doing that makes our offering
something beautiful for God.

MOTHER TERESA

A cup that is already full cannot have more added to
it. In order to receive the further good to which
we are entitled, we must give of that which we have.

MARGARET BECKER

A cheerful giver does not count the cost of
what he gives. His heart is set on pleasing and
cheering him to whom the gift is given.

JULIANA OF NORWICH

How can we withhold from another what
God has so generously allowed us to use and enjoy?

JAN WINEBRENNER

MORE FROM GOD'S WORD

The good person is generous and lends lavishly . . . .

PSALM 112:5 MSG

Freely you have received, freely give.

MATTHEW 10:8 NKJV

TODAY, I WILL THINK ABOUT . . .

Ways that I can be more generous with my
possessions, my talents, my time, and my love.

A PRAYER TO START MY DAY

Father, Your gifts are priceless. You gave Your Son
Jesus to save us, and Your motivation was love.
I pray that the gifts I give to others will
come from an overflow of my heart,
and that they will echo the great love
You have for all of Your children. **Amen

FORGIVENESS TODAY

STOP JUDGING OTHERS,
AND YOU WILL NOT BE JUDGED.
STOP CRITICIZING OTHERS,
OR IT WILL ALL COME BACK ON YOU.
IF YOU FORGIVE OTHERS,
YOU WILL BE FORGIVEN.

LUKE 6:37 NLT

Even the most mild-mannered women will, on occasion, have reason to become angry with the inevitable shortcomings of family members and friends. But wise women are quick to forgive others, just as God has forgiven them.

The commandment to forgive others is clearly a part of God's Word, but oh how difficult a commandment it can be to follow. Because we are imperfect beings, we are quick to anger, quick to blame, slow to forgive, and even slower to forget. No matter. Even when forgiveness is difficult, God's instructions are straightforward: As Christians who have received the gift of forgiveness, we must now share that gift with others.

If, in your heart, you hold bitterness against even a single person, forgive. If there exists even one person, alive or dead, whom you have not forgiven, follow God's commandment and His will for your life: forgive. If you are embittered against yourself for some past mistake or shortcoming, forgive. Then, to the best of your abilities, forget, and move on. Then, when you've forgiven others, you can turn your thoughts to a far more pleasant subject: the incredibly bright future that God has promised.

Only God in Christ has the power to forgive sin.
But you and I must confess it to Him personally,
specifically, and honestly if we want
to receive forgiveness.

ANNE GRAHAM LOTZ

Forgiveness does not mean the perpetrator goes free;
it means that the forgiver is free and that God will
justly deal with those who have caused pain.

CYNTHIA HEALD

There is nothing, absolutely nothing, that God will
not forgive. You cannot "out-sin" His forgiveness.
You cannot "out-sin" the love of God.

KATHY TROCCOLI

Have you thought that your willingness to forgive is
really your affirmation of the power of God
to do you good?

PAULA RINEHART

MORE FROM GOD'S WORD

*Be kind to one another, tender-hearted, forgiving
each other, just as God in Christ also has forgiven you.*

EPHESIANS 4:32 NASB

*Those who show mercy to others are happy,
because God will show mercy to them.*

MATTHEW 5:7 NCV

TODAY, I WILL THINK ABOUT . . .

The people whom I still need to forgive.

A PRAYER TO START MY DAY

Lord, make me a woman who is slow to anger and
quick to forgive. When I am bitter, You can change
my unforgiving heart. And, when I am angry,
Your Word reminds me that forgiveness is
Your commandment. Let me be Your obedient
servant, Lord, and let me forgive others
just as You have forgiven me. **Amen

A TIME FOR RENEWAL

I WILL GIVE YOU A NEW HEART
AND PUT A NEW SPIRIT IN YOU . . . .

EZEKIEL 36:26 NIV

For busy women living in a fast-paced 21st-century world, life may seem like a merry-go-round that never stops turning. If that description seems to fit your life, then you may find yourself running short of patience or strength or both. If you're feeling tired or discouraged, there is a source from which you can draw the power needed to recharge your spiritual batteries. That source is God.

Are you exhausted or troubled? Turn your heart toward God in prayer. Are you weak or worried? Take the time—or, more accurately, make the time—to delve deeply into God's Holy Word. Are you spiritually depleted? Call upon fellow believers to support you, and call upon Christ to renew your spirit and your life. When you do, you'll discover that the Creator of the universe stands always ready and always able to create a new sense of wonderment and joy in you.

He is the God of wholeness and restoration.

STORMIE OMARTIAN

With God, it's never "Plan B" or "second best."
It's always "Plan A." And, if we let Him,
He'll make something beautiful of our lives.

GLORIA GAITHER

In those desperate times when we feel like we don't
have an ounce of strength, He will gently pick up
our heads so that our eyes can behold something—
something that will keep His hope alive in us.

KATHY TROCCOLI

But while relaxation is one thing, refreshment is
another. We need to drink frequently and
at length from God's fresh springs, to spend time in
the Scripture, time in fellowship with Him,
time worshiping Him.

RUTH BELL GRAHAM

Repentance removes old sins and wrong attitudes,
and it opens the way for the Holy Spirit
to restore our spiritual health.

SHIRLEY DOBSON

MORE FROM GOD'S WORD

. . . inwardly we are being renewed day by day.

2 CORINTHIANS 4:16 NIV

*"For I will restore health to you and heal you
of your wounds," says the L*ORD.

JEREMIAH 30:17 NKJV

TODAY, I WILL THINK ABOUT . . .

The strength that can be mine when I allow
Christ to dwell in the center of my heart.

A PRAYER TO START MY DAY

Lord, I am an imperfect woman. Because my faith is
limited, I may become overwhelmed by the demands
of the day. When I feel tired or discouraged,
renew my strength. When I am worried, let me turn
my thoughts and my prayers to You. Let me trust
Your promises, dear Lord, and let me accept
Your unending love, now and forever. **Amen

SENSING GOD'S PRESENCE TODAY

DRAW NEAR TO GOD,
AND HE WILL DRAW NEAR TO YOU.

JAMES 4:8 HCSB

Since God is everywhere, we are free to sense His presence whenever we take the time to quiet our souls and turn our prayers to Him. But sometimes, amid the incessant demands of everyday life, we turn our thoughts far from God; when we do, we suffer.

Do you set aside quiet moments each day to offer praise to your Creator? As a woman who has received the gift of God's grace, you most certainly should. Silence is a gift that you give to yourself and to God. During these moments of stillness, you will often sense the infinite love and power of your Creator—and He, in turn, will speak directly to your heart.

The familiar words of Psalm 46:10 remind us to "Be still, and know that I am God." When we do so, we encounter the awesome presence of our loving Heavenly Father, and we are comforted in the knowledge that God is not just near. He is here.

I think we Christians have become lazy.
We would rather read a book about how someone
else became closer to God than spend time alone
with him ourselves.

SHEILA WALSH

As I wander from village to village, I feel it is
no idle fancy that the Master walks beside me and
I hear his voice saying gently,
"I am with you always, even unto the end."

LOTTIE MOON, MISSIONARY

It is God to whom and with whom we travel,
and while He is the End of our journey,
He is also at every stopping place.

ELISABETH ELLIOT

The love of God is so vast, the power of his touch
so invigorating, we could just stay in his presence for
hours, soaking up his glory, basking in his blessings.

DEBRA EVANS

The tender eyes of God perpetually see us.
He has never stopped noticing.

ANGELA THOMAS

MORE FROM GOD'S WORD

*For the eyes of the LORD range throughout
the earth to strengthen those whose hearts
are fully committed to him.*

2 CHRONICLES 16:9 NIV

TODAY, I WILL THINK ABOUT . . .

The need to seek God's presence and the wisdom of
allowing God to influence my decisions
throughout the day.

A PRAYER TO START MY DAY

Dear Lord, You are with me always. Help me
feel Your presence in every situation and every
circumstance. Today, dear God, let me feel You
and acknowledge Your presence, Your love,
and Your Son. **Amen

BEYOND BUSYNESS

CAREFUL PLANNING PUTS YOU AHEAD
IN THE LONG RUN; HURRY AND SCURRY
PUTS YOU FURTHER BEHIND.

PROVERBS 21:5 MSG

How much time do you spend getting to know God? A lot? A little? Almost none? The answer to this question will help determine the state of your spiritual health. And make no mistake: the more time and energy you invest with God, the better you'll come to know Him.

Are you carving out enough time each day to praise God and to study His Word? If so, you know firsthand the blessings that He offers those who worship Him consistently and sincerely. But, if you have unintentionally allowed the hustle and bustle of your busy day to come between you and your Creator, then you must slow down, take a deep breath, and rearrange your priorities.

God loved this world so much that He sent His Son to save it. And now only one real question remains for you: what will you do in response to God's love? The answer should be obvious: God must come first in your life. He is the Giver of all good things, and He is the One who sent His Son so that you might have eternal life. He deserves your prayers, your obedience, your stewardship, and your love—and He deserves these things all day every day, not just on Sunday mornings.

It's ironic that one of the best remedies for
impending burnout is to give yourself away—
to pick out one time and place each week where
you can stretch out your hands for
the pure joy of doing it.

LIZ CURTIS HIGGS

When I am constantly running there is
no time for being. When there is no time
for being there is no time for listening.

MADELEINE L'ENGLE

If you can't seem to find time for God,
then you're simply too busy for your own good.
God is never too busy for you,
and you should never be too busy for Him.

MARIE T. FREEMAN

Frustration is not the will of God.
There is time to do anything and everything
that God wants us to do.

ELISABETH ELLIOT

MORE FROM GOD'S WORD

I said to myself, "Relax and rest.
God has showered you with blessings."

PSALM 116:7 MSG

TODAY, I WILL THINK ABOUT . . .

The importance of doing first things first *and*
the importance of putting God first.

A PRAYER TO START MY DAY

Dear Lord, when the quickening pace of life leaves
me with little time for worship or for praise,
help me to reorder my priorities. When the demands
of the day leave me distracted and discouraged,
let me turn to Jesus for the peace that only He can
give. And then, when I have accepted the spiritual
abundance that is mine through Christ,
let me share His message and His love
with all who cross my path. **Amen

THE RIGHT KIND OF EXAMPLE

YOU SHOULD BE AN EXAMPLE
TO THE BELIEVERS IN SPEECH, IN CONDUCT,
IN LOVE, IN FAITH, IN PURITY.

1 TIMOTHY 4:12 HCSB

Whether we like it or not, all of us are role models. Our friends and family members watch our actions and, as followers of Christ, we are obliged to act accordingly.

What kind of example are you? Are you the kind of woman whose life serves as a genuine example of righteousness? Are you a woman whose behavior serves as a positive role model for young people? Are you the kind of woman whose actions, day in and day out, are based upon kindness, faithfulness, and a love for the Lord? If so, you are not only blessed by God, you are also a powerful force for good in a world that desperately needs positive influences such as yours.

Corrie ten Boom advised, "Don't worry about what you do not understand. Worry about what you do understand in the Bible but do not live by." And that's sound advice because our families and friends are watching . . . and so, for that matter, is God.

There is a transcendent power in example.
We reform others unconsciously
when we walk uprightly.

ANNE SOPHIE SWETCHINE

We must mirror God's love in the midst of
a world full of hatred. We are the mirrors of
God's love, so we may show Jesus by our lives.

CORRIE TEN BOOM

I'd rather see a sermon than hear one any day;
I'd rather one should walk with me
than merely tell the way.

EDGAR A. GUEST

"I read about it in the Bible" is true and good.
Yet, "I have seen him with the eyes of my heart"
is often more convincing. And convicting.

LIZ CURTIS HIGGS

Any child will learn to worship God who lives
his daily life with adults who worship Him.

ANNA B. MOW

MORE FROM GOD'S WORD

In everything set them an example by doing what is good.

TITUS 2:7 NIV

You are the light that gives light to the world. In the same way, you should be a light for other people. Live so that they will see the good things you do and will praise your Father in heaven.

MATTHEW 5:14,16 NCV

TODAY, I WILL THINK ABOUT . . .

Ways that my own behavior impacts my family and friends.

A PRAYER TO START MY DAY

Dear Lord, help me be a worthy example to my friends and to my family. Let the things that I say and the things that I do show everyone what it means to be a follower of Your Son. **Amen

A WOMAN OF INTEGRITY

THE GODLY WALK WITH INTEGRITY;
BLESSED ARE THEIR CHILDREN AFTER THEM.

PROVERBS 20:7 NLT

Wise women understand that integrity is a crucial building block in the foundation of a well-lived life. Integrity is built slowly over a lifetime. It is the sum of every right decision, every honest word, every noble thought, and every heartfelt prayer. It is forged on the anvil of honorable work and polished by the twin virtues of generosity and humility. Integrity is a precious thing—difficult to build, but easy to tear down; godly women value it and protect it at all costs.

As believers in Christ, we must seek to live each day with discipline, honesty, and faith. When we do, at least two things happen: integrity becomes a habit, and God blesses us because of our obedience to Him.

Living a life of integrity isn't always the easiest way, but it is always the right way. And God clearly intends that it should be our way, too.

God never called us to naïveté. He called us
to integrity . . . . The biblical concept of integrity
emphasizes mature innocence not childlike
ignorance.

BETH MOORE

Integrity is the glue that holds our way of
life together. We must constantly strive to keep
our integrity intact. When wealth is lost,
nothing is lost; when health is lost,
something is lost; when character is lost, all is lost.

BILLY GRAHAM

Be honorable yourself if you wish to associate
with honorable people.

WELSH PROVERB

Character cannot be developed in ease and quiet.
Only through experience of trial and suffering can
the soul be strengthened, vision cleared,
ambition inspired, and success achieved.

HELEN KELLER

Integrity of heart is indispensable.

JOHN CALVIN

MORE FROM GOD'S WORD

People with integrity have firm footing,
but those who follow crooked paths will slip and fall.

PROVERBS 10:9 NLT

Good people will be guided by honesty;
dishonesty will destroy those who are not trustworthy.

PROVERBS 11:3 NCV

TODAY, I WILL THINK ABOUT . . .

Ways that I can remove myself from situations
that might compromise my integrity.

A PRAYER TO START MY DAY

Lord, You are a God of truth; let me be a woman of
truth. Sometimes speaking the truth is difficult,
but when I am weak or fearful, give me the strength
to speak words that are worthy of the One who
created me, so that others might see Your eternal
truth reflected in my words and my deeds. **Amen

THE ATTITUDE YOU CHOOSE

AND NOW, DEAR BROTHERS AND SISTERS,
LET ME SAY ONE MORE THING AS I CLOSE
THIS LETTER. FIX YOUR THOUGHTS ON WHAT IS
TRUE AND HONORABLE AND RIGHT.
THINK ABOUT THINGS THAT ARE PURE AND
LOVELY AND ADMIRABLE. THINK ABOUT THINGS
THAT ARE EXCELLENT AND WORTHY OF PRAISE.

PHILIPPIANS 4:8 NLT

As a Christian woman, you have every reason to rejoice. God is in His heaven; Christ has risen, and you are God's child. But, when the demands of life seem great and our resources seem small by comparison, you may become exhausted, discouraged, or both.

As you plan for the day ahead, here's a question to consider: What will your attitude be today? Will you be fearful, angry, or worried? Will you be bitter or pessimistic? Will you be sarcastic or cynical? If so, God wants to have a little chat with you.

God created you in His own image, and He wants you to experience His joy and abundance. But, God will not force His joy upon you; you must claim it for yourself. So today, and every day hereafter, celebrate this life that God has given you. Think optimistically about yourself and your future. Give thanks to the One who has given you everything, and trust in your heart that He wants to give you so much more.

The things we think are the things that feed
our souls. If we think on pure and lovely things,
we shall grow pure and lovely like them;
and the converse is equally true.

HANNAH WHITALL SMITH

The greater part of our happiness or misery depends
on our dispositions, and not on our circumstances.

MARTHA WASHINGTON

The Reference Point for the Christian is the Bible.
All values, judgments, and attitudes must be gauged
in relationship to this Reference Point.

RUTH BELL GRAHAM

You must do the thing you think you cannot do.

ELEANOR ROOSEVELT

Keep your face to the sunshine,
and you cannot see the shadows.

HELEN KELLER

MORE FROM GOD'S WORD

A miserable heart means a miserable life;
a cheerful heart fills the day with a song.

PROVERBS 15:15 MSG

Your attitude should be the same
that Christ Jesus had.

PHILIPPIANS 2:5 NLT

TODAY, I WILL THINK ABOUT . . .

The importance of focusing my thoughts on
the positive aspects of life, not the negative ones.

A PRAYER TO START MY DAY

Lord, I have so many reasons to be thankful;
let my attitude be a reflection of the many blessings
I have received. Make me a woman whose thoughts
are Christlike and whose hopes are worthy of
the One who has given me so much. **Amen

THE WILLINGNESS TO HELP

THE ONE WHO BLESSES OTHERS IS
ABUNDANTLY BLESSED;
THOSE WHO HELP OTHERS ARE HELPED.

PROVERBS 11:25 MSG

Neighbors. We know that we are instructed to love them, and yet there's so little time . . . and we're so busy. No matter. As Christians, we are commanded by our Lord and Savior Jesus Christ to love our neighbors just as we love ourselves. We are not asked to love our neighbors, nor are we encouraged to do so. We are commanded to love them. Period.

In order to love our neighbors as God intends, we must first slow down long enough to understand their needs. Slowing down, however, is not as simple as it seems. We live in a fast-paced world with pressures and demands that often sap our time and our energy. Sometimes, we may convince ourselves that slowing down is not an option, but when we do so, we are wrong. Caring for our neighbors must be *our* priority because it is *God's* priority.

This very day, you will encounter someone who needs a word of encouragement or a pat on the back or a helping hand or a heartfelt prayer. And, if you don't reach out to your friends, who will? If you don't take the time to understand the needs of your neighbors, who will? If you don't love your brothers and sisters, who will? So, today, look for a neighbor in need . . . and then do something to help. Father's orders.

I never look at the masses as my responsibility.
I look at the individual. I can love only one person
at a time. I can feed only one person at a time.
Just one, one, one. You get closer to Christ by
coming closer to each other.

MOTHER TERESA

Do all the good you can. By all the means you can.
In all the ways you can. In all the places you can.
At all the times you can. To all the people you can.
As long as ever you can.

JOHN WESLEY

How wonderful it is that nobody need wait
a single moment before starting to improve
the world.

ANNE FRANK

What this old world needs is less advice and
more helping hands.

ANONYMOUS

MORE FROM GOD'S WORD

Then a Samaritan traveling down the road came to where the hurt man was. When he saw the man, he felt very sorry for him. The Samaritan went to him, poured olive oil and wine on his wounds, and bandaged them. Then he put the hurt man on his own donkey and took him to an inn where he cared for him.

LUKE 10:33-34 NCV

TODAY, I WILL THINK ABOUT . . .

A creative way to lend a helping hand to someone nearby.

A PRAYER TO START MY DAY

Dear Lord, let me help others in every way that I can. Jesus served others; I can too. I will serve other people with my good deeds and with my prayers, today and every day. **Amen

SHARING YOUR TESTIMONY

FOR GOD HAS NOT GIVEN US A SPIRIT OF FEAR
AND TIMIDITY, BUT OF POWER, LOVE,
AND SELF-DISCIPLINE. SO YOU MUST
NEVER BE ASHAMED TO TELL OTHERS
ABOUT OUR LORD.

2 TIMOTHY 1:7-8 NLT

In his second letter to Timothy, Paul offers a message to believers of every generation when he writes, "God has not given us a spirit of timidity" (1:7). Paul's meaning is crystal clear: When sharing our testimonies, we, as Christians, must be courageous, forthright, and unashamed.

We live in a world that desperately needs the healing message of Christ Jesus. Every believer, each in his or her own way, bears responsibility for sharing the Good News of our Savior. It is important to remember that we bear testimony through both words and actions. Wise Christians follow the admonition of St. Francis of Assisi who advised, "Preach the gospel at all times and, if necessary, use words."

If you are a believer in Christ, you know how He has touched your heart and changed your life. Now is the time to share your testimony with others. So, as you make plans for the coming day, look for ways to preach the Gospel with your words *and* your deeds . . . but not necessarily in that order.

Claim the joy that is yours. Pray.
And know that your joy is used by God
to reach others.

KAY ARTHUR

Faith in small things has repercussions that ripple
all the way out. In a huge, dark room
a little match can light up the place.

JONI EARECKSON TADA

There are many timid souls whom we jostle morning
and evening as we pass them by;
but if only the kind word were spoken they might
become fully persuaded.

FANNY CROSBY

When people share their experience of
transformation, crediting the living, loving God
with their visible, tangible change, this validates
faith and allows others to hope, search, and find that
God is powerful, present, and personal in our time.

BECKY TIRABASSI

MORE FROM GOD'S WORD

*All those who stand before others and say they believe
in me, I will say before my Father in heaven
that they belong to me.*

MATTHEW 10:32 NCV

*Be wise in the way you act with people who
are not believers, making the most of every opportunity.*

COLOSSIANS 4:5 NCV

TODAY, I WILL THINK ABOUT . . .

The importance of sharing my testimony through
my words *and* my actions.

A PRAYER TO START MY DAY

Lord, the life that I live and the words that
I speak will tell the world how I feel about You.
Today and every day, let my testimony be worthy
of You. Let my words be sure and true,
and let my actions point others to You. **Amen

EXPERIENCING THE JOY

ALWAYS BE FULL OF JOY IN THE LORD.

I SAY IT AGAIN—REJOICE!

PHILIPPIANS 4:4 NLT

God's Word makes it clear: He intends that His joy should become our joy. The Lord intends that believers should share His love with His joy in their hearts. Yet sometimes, amid the inevitable hustle and bustle of life here on earth, we can forfeit—albeit temporarily—God's joy as we wrestle with the challenges of daily living.

Joni Eareckson Tada spoke for Christian women of every generation when she observed, "I wanted the deepest part of me to vibrate with that ancient yet familiar longing, that desire for something that would fill and overflow my soul."

Psalm 100 reminds us that, as believers, we have every reason to celebrate: "Shout for joy to the LORD, all the earth. Worship the LORD with gladness" (vv. 1-2 NIV). These words most certainly apply to you.

Are you a woman whose joy is clearly evident to your family and friends? If so, congratulations—you're doing God's will. But, if you find yourself feeling discouraged or worse, it's time to slow down and have a quiet conversation with your Creator.

If your heart is heavy, turn to Christ. He will give you peace and joy. And if you already have the joy of Christ in your heart, share it freely, just as Christ has freely shared His joy with you.

O the precious name of Jesus!
How it thrills our souls with joy.

LYDIA BAXTER

If you're a thinking Christian,
you will be a joyful Christian.

MARIE T. FREEMAN

It is the definition of joy to be able to offer back to
God the essence of what he's placed in you,
be that creativity or a love of ideas or
a compassionate heart or the gift of hospitality.

PAULA RINEHART

Finding joy means first of all finding Jesus.

JILL BRISCOE

Every morning is a fresh opportunity to find
God's extraordinary joy in the most ordinary places.

JANET. L. WEAVER

MORE FROM GOD'S WORD

So now we can rejoice in our wonderful new relationship with God—all because of what our Lord Jesus Christ has done for us in making us friends of God.

ROMANS 5:11 NLT

O clap your hands, all peoples;
Shout to God with the voice of joy.

PSALM 47:1 NASB

TODAY, I WILL THINK ABOUT . . .

The impact that my emotions have on other people.

A PRAYER TO START MY DAY

Lord, You have told me to give thanks always and to rejoice in Your marvelous creation. Let me be a joyful Christian, Lord, and let me focus my thoughts upon Your blessings and Your love. Help me make this day and every day a cause for celebration as I share the Good News of Your Son Jesus. **Amen

MAKING TIME FOR SILENCE

BE STILL, AND KNOW THAT I AM GOD.

PSALM 46:10 NKJV

The world seems to grow louder day by day, and our senses seem to be invaded at every turn. But, if we allow the distractions of a clamorous society to separate us from God's peace, we do ourselves a profound disservice. Our task, as dutiful believers, is to carve out moments of silence in a world filled with noise.

If we are to maintain righteous minds and compassionate hearts, we must take time each day for prayer and for meditation. We must make ourselves still in the presence of our Creator. We must quiet our minds and our hearts so that we might sense God's will and His love.

Has the busy pace of life robbed you of the peace that God has promised? If so, it's time to reorder your priorities and your life. Nothing is more important than the time you spend with your Heavenly Father. So, as you make plans for the day ahead, make time for quiet moments with God. Be still and claim the inner peace that is found in the silent moments you spend with your Creator. His peace is offered freely; it has been paid for in full; it is yours for the asking. So ask. And then share.

Be still, and in the quiet moments
listen to the voice of your heavenly Father.
His words can renew your spirit.
No one knows you and your needs like He does.

JANET L. WEAVER

When an honest soul can get still before the living
Christ, we can still hear Him say simply and clearly,
"Love the Lord your God with all your heart and
with all your soul and with all your mind . . .
and love one another as I have loved you."

GLORIA GAITHER

The world is full of noise. Might we not set ourselves
to learn silence, stillness, solitude?

ELISABETH ELLIOT

Because Jesus Christ is our Great High Priest,
not only can we approach God without a human
"go-between," we can also hear and learn from God
in some sacred moments without one.

BETH MOORE

MORE FROM GOD'S WORD

I wait quietly before God,
for my salvation comes from him.

PSALM 62:1 NLT

TODAY, I WILL THINK ABOUT . . .

The importance of silence.

Silence is okay:
Sometimes, just being there is enough.
If you're not sure what to say,
it's okay to say nothing.

A PRAYER TO START MY DAY

Dear Lord, in the quiet moments of this day,
I will turn my thoughts and prayers to You. In these
silent moments, I will sense Your presence,
and I will seek Your will for my life, knowing that
when I accept Your peace, I will be blessed
today and throughout eternity. **Amen

THE POWER OF FAITH

I TELL YOU THE TRUTH, IF YOU HAVE FAITH
AND DO NOT DOUBT . . . . YOU CAN SAY TO
THIS MOUNTAIN "GO AND THROW YOURSELF
INTO THE SEA," AND IT WILL BE DONE.

MATTHEW 21:21 NIV

When a suffering woman sought healing by simply touching the hem of His garment, Jesus turned and said, "Daughter, be of good comfort; thy faith hath made thee whole" (Matthew 9:22 KJV). We, too, can be made whole when we place our faith completely and unwaveringly in the person of Jesus Christ.

Concentration camp survivor Corrie ten Boom relied on faith during her ten months of imprisonment and torture. Later, despite the fact that four of her family members had died in Nazi death camps, Corrie's faith was unshaken. She wrote, "There is no pit so deep that God's love is not deeper still." Christians take note: Genuine faith in God means faith in all circumstances, happy or sad, joyful or tragic.

If your faith is being tested to the point of breaking, know that Your Savior is near. If you reach out to Him in faith, He will give you peace and heal your broken spirit. Be content to touch even the smallest fragment of the Master's garment, and He will make you whole.

Faith is putting all your eggs in God's basket,
then counting your blessings before they hatch.

RAMONA C. CARROLL

Faith does not concern itself with the entire journey.
One step is enough.

MRS. CHARLES E. COWMAN

Faith is not just believing; faith is being open to
what God is doing, being willing to learn and grow.

MARY MORRISON SUGGS

Let me encourage you to continue to wait
with faith. God may not perform a miracle,
but He is trustworthy to touch you and
make you whole where there used to be a hole.

LISA WHELCHEL

Faith is our spiritual oxygen.
It not only keeps us alive in God,
but enables us to grow stronger . . . .

JOYCE LANDORF HEATHERLY

MORE FROM GOD'S WORD

*The fundamental fact of existence is that
this trust in God, this faith, is the firm foundation under
everything that makes life worth living.*

HEBREWS 11:1 MSG

Now the just shall live by faith.

HEBREWS 10:38 NKJV

TODAY, I WILL THINK ABOUT . . .

The importance of trusting God *and*
the strength that comes from trusting God.

A PRAYER TO START MY DAY

Dear Lord, help me to be a woman of faith.
Help me to remember that You are always near and
that You can overcome any challenge.
With Your love and Your power, Lord,
I can live courageously and faithfully
today and every day. **Amen

ACCEPTING GOD'S SPIRITUAL ABUNDANCE

I CAME THAT THEY MAY HAVE LIFE,
AND HAVE IT ABUNDANTLY.

JOHN 10:10 NASB

The familiar words of John 10:10 should serve as a daily reminder: Christ came to this earth so that we might experience His abundance, His love, and His gift of eternal life. But Christ does not force Himself upon us; we must claim His gifts for ourselves.

Every woman knows that some days are so busy and so hurried that abundance seems a distant promise. It is not. Every day, we can claim the spiritual abundance that God promises for our lives . . . and we should.

Hannah Whitall Smith spoke for believers of every generation when she observed, "God is the giver, and we are the receivers. And His richest gifts are bestowed not upon those who do the greatest things, but upon those who accept His abundance and His grace."

Christ is, indeed, the Giver. Will you accept His gifts today?

The gift of God is eternal life, spiritual life,
abundant life through faith in Jesus Christ,
the Living Word of God.

ANNE GRAHAM LOTZ

It would be wrong to have a "poverty complex,"
for to think ourselves paupers is to deny either
the King's riches or to deny our being His children.

CATHERINE MARSHALL

We do not need to beg Him to bless us;
He simply cannot help it.

HANNAH WHITALL SMITH

Jesus intended for us to be overwhelmed by
the blessings of regular days. He said it was
the reason he had come: "I am come that they
might have life, and that they might have it
more abundantly."

GLORIA GAITHER

MORE FROM GOD'S WORD

And God will generously provide all you need.
Then you will always have everything you need and
plenty left over to share with others.

2 CORINTHIANS 9:8 NLT

TODAY, I WILL THINK ABOUT . . .

The spiritual abundance that can be mine in Christ.

A PRAYER TO START MY DAY

Dear Lord, thank You for the joyful, abundant
life that is mine through Christ Jesus. Guide me
according to Your will, and help me become
a woman whose life is a worthy example to others.
Give me courage, Lord, to claim the spiritual riches
that You have promised, and show me
Your plan for my life, today and forever. **Amen

PRIORITIES THAT ARE PLEASING TO GOD

THE THING YOU SHOULD WANT MOST IS
GOD'S KINGDOM AND DOING WHAT
GOD WANTS. THEN ALL THESE OTHER THINGS
YOU NEED WILL BE GIVEN TO YOU.

MATTHEW 6:33 NCV

When God made you, He equipped you with an array of talents and abilities that are uniquely yours. It's up to you to discover those talents and to use them, but sometimes the world will encourage you to do otherwise. At times, society will attempt to cubbyhole you, to standardize you, and to make you fit into a particular, preformed mold. Perhaps God has other plans.

Sometimes, because you're an imperfect human being, you may become so wrapped up in meeting society's expectations that you fail to focus on God's expectations. To do so is a mistake of major proportions—don't make it. Instead, seek God's guidance as you focus your energies on becoming the person God wants you to be.

As you make plans for the upcoming day, how do you intend to use the talents God has given you? Will you seek to please God or man? Your primary obligation is not to please imperfect men and women. Your obligation is to strive diligently to meet the expectations of an all-knowing and perfect God. Trust Him always. Love Him always. Praise Him always. And seek to please Him. Always.

If you are receiving your affirmation, love,
self-worth, joy, strength and acceptance
from anywhere but God, He will shake it.

LISA BEVERE

Make God's will the focus of your life day by day.
If you seek to please Him and Him alone,
you'll find yourself satisfied with life.

KAY ARTHUR

If you really want to please God and intend to be
in full agreement with His will, you can't go wrong.

FRANCIS MARY PAUL LIBERMANN

Get ready for God to show you not only
His pleasure, but His approval.

JONI EARECKSON TADA

We shouldn't work towards being saints,
but to please God.

ST. THÉRÈSE OF LISIEUX

MORE FROM GOD'S WORD

But neither exile nor homecoming is the main thing.
Cheerfully pleasing God is the main thing, and
that's what we aim to do, regardless of our conditions.

2 CORINTHIANS 5:9 MSG

TODAY, I WILL THINK ABOUT . . .

The importance of living a life that is
pleasing to God.

A PRAYER TO START MY DAY

Dear Lord, today I will honor You with my thoughts,
my actions, and my prayers. I will seek to please You,
and I will strive to serve You. Your blessings are
as limitless as Your love. And because I have been
so richly blessed, I will worship You, Father,
with thanksgiving in my heart and praise on my lips,
this day and forever. **Amen

A DAY OF PRAYER

REJOICE ALWAYS, PRAY WITHOUT CEASING,
IN EVERYTHING GIVE THANKS;
FOR THIS IS THE WILL OF GOD
IN CHRIST JESUS FOR YOU.

1 THESSALONIANS 5:16-18 NKJV

On his second missionary journey, Paul started a small church in Thessalonica. A short time later, he penned a letter that was intended to encourage the new believers at that church. Today, almost 2,000 years later, 1 Thessalonians remains a powerful, practical guide for Christian living.

In his letter, Paul advised members of the new church to "pray without ceasing." His advice applies to Christians of every generation. When we consult God on an hourly basis, we avail ourselves of His wisdom, His strength, and His love. As Corrie ten Boom observed, "Any concern that is too small to be turned into a prayer is too small to be made into a burden."

Make today a day of prayer. Today, instead of turning things over in your mind, turn them over to God in prayer. Instead of worrying about your next decision, ask God to lead the way. Don't limit your prayers to meals or bedtime. Become a woman of constant prayer. God is listening, and He wants to hear from you. Now.

Always stay connected to people and seek out things
that bring you joy. Dream with abandon.
Pray confidently.

BARBARA JOHNSON

I have found the perfect antidote for fear.
Whenever it sticks up its ugly face,
I clobber it with prayer.

DALE EVANS ROGERS

We must pray literally without ceasing,
in every occurrence and employment of our lives.
You know I mean that prayer of the heart which
is independent of place or situation, or which is,
rather, a habit of lifting up the heart to God,
as in a constant communication with Him.

ST. ELIZABETH ANN SETON

Prayer is a long rope with a strong hold.

HARRIET BEECHER STOWE

There is nothing surer on this earth than
the truth that God hears and answers prayers.

LEANNE PAYNE

MORE FROM GOD'S WORD

*If my people who are called by my name,
will humble themselves and pray and seek my face
and turn from their wicked ways, then will I hear from
heaven and will forgive their sin and will heal their land.*

2 CHRONICLES 7:14 NIV

The intense prayer of the righteous is very powerful.

JAMES 5:16 HCSB

TODAY, I WILL THINK ABOUT . . .

The role that prayer plays in my life.

A PRAYER TO START MY DAY

Dear Lord, I will be a woman of prayer.
I will take everything to You in prayer,
and when I do, I will trust Your answers. **Amen

CHEERFULNESS IN THE HERE AND NOW

A CHEERFUL HEART IS GOOD MEDICINE.

PROVERBS 17:22 NIV

On some days, as every woman knows, it's hard to be cheerful. Sometimes, as the demands of the world increase and our energy sags, we feel less like "cheering up" and more like "tearing up." But even in our darkest hours, we can turn to God, and He will give us comfort.

Few things in life are more sad, or, for that matter, more absurd, than a grumpy Christian. Christ promises us lives of abundance and joy, but He does not force His joy upon us. We must claim His joy for ourselves, and when we do, Jesus, in turn, fills our spirits with His power and His love.

How can we receive from Christ the joy that is rightfully ours? By giving Him what is rightfully His: our hearts and our souls.

When we earnestly commit ourselves to the Savior of mankind, when we place Jesus at the center of our lives and trust Him as our personal Savior, He will transform us, not just for today, but for all eternity. Then we, as God's children, can share Christ's joy and His message with a world that needs both.

The greatest honor you can give Almighty God is
to live gladly and joyfully because of
the knowledge of His love.

JULIANA OF NORWICH

God is good, and heaven is forever.
And if those two facts don't cheer you up,
nothing will.

MARIE T. FREEMAN

Cheerfulness prepares a glorious mind for all
the noblest acts of religion—love, adoration,
praise, and every union with our God.

ST. ELIZABETH ANN SETON

A sad nun is a bad nun; I am more afraid of
one unhappy sister than of a crowd of evil spirits.

ST. TERESA OF AVILA

Be merry, really merry. The life of a true Christian
should be a perpetual jubilee,
a prelude to the festivals of eternity.

THEOPHARE VENARD

MORE FROM GOD'S WORD

A happy heart is like a continual feast.

PROVERBS 15:15 NCV

Jacob said, "For what a relief it is to see your friendly smile. It is like seeing the smile of God!"

GENESIS 33:10 NLT

TODAY, I WILL THINK ABOUT . . .

The impact of my cheerfulness on others.

A PRAYER TO START MY DAY

Dear Lord, You have given me so many reasons
to be cheerful. Today, let me be a joyful Christian,
quick to smile and slow to frown.
And, let Your love shine in me and through me,
this day and forever. **Amen

TAKING TIME TO ENCOURAGE OTHERS

WATCH THE WAY YOU TALK.
LET NOTHING FOUL OR DIRTY COME OUT
OF YOUR MOUTH. SAY ONLY WHAT HELPS,
EACH WORD A GIFT.

EPHESIANS 4:29 MSG

Are you a woman who is a continuing source of encouragement to your family and friends? Hopefully so. After all, one of the reasons that God put you here is to serve and encourage other people—starting with the people who live under your roof.

In his letter to the Ephesians, Paul writes, "Do not let any unwholesome talk come out of your mouths, but only what is helpful for building others up according to their needs, that it may benefit those who listen" (vv. 29 NIV). This passage reminds us that, as Christians, we are instructed to choose our words carefully so as to build others up through wholesome, honest encouragement. How can we build others up? By celebrating their victories and their accomplishments. As the old saying goes, "When someone does something good, applaud— you'll make two people happy."

Today, look for the good in others and celebrate the good that you find. When you do, you'll be a powerful force of encouragement in your corner of the world . . . and a worthy servant to your God.

The overall goal in helping any individual is
to communicate hope, that they might more
courageously and confidently face daily life
with its trials and struggles.

VERNA BIRKEY

If someone listens or stretches out a hand or
whispers a word of encouragement or
attempts to understand a lonely person,
extraordinary things begin to happen.

LORETTA GIRZARTIS

So often we think that to be encouragers we have to
produce great words of wisdom when, in fact,
a few simple syllables of sympathy and
an arm around the shoulder can often provide
much needed comfort.

FLORENCE LITTAUER

My special friends, who know me so well and
love me anyway, give me daily encouragement
to keep on.

EMILIE BARNES

MORE FROM GOD'S WORD

Patience and encouragement come from God.
And I pray that God will help you all agree
with each other the way Christ Jesus wants.

ROMANS 15:5 NCV

TODAY, I WILL THINK ABOUT . . .

The impact that my encouragement
has upon others.

A PRAYER TO START MY DAY

Dear Lord, because I am Your child, I am blessed.
You have loved me eternally, cared for me faithfully,
and saved me through the gift of Your Son Jesus.
Just as You have lifted me up, Lord, let me lift up
others in a spirit of encouragement and hope.
And, if I can help even a single person, Lord,
may the glory be Yours. **Amen

WHEN THE DAY IS DIFFICULT

JESUS SAID, "DON'T LET YOUR HEARTS
BE TROUBLED. TRUST IN GOD,
AND TRUST IN ME."

JOHN 14:1 NCV

Face facts: the upcoming day will *not* be problem-free. In fact, your life can be viewed as an exercise in problem-solving. The question is not whether you will encounter problems; the real question is how you will choose to address them.

When it comes to solving the problems of everyday living, we often know precisely what needs to be done, but we may be slow in doing it—especially if what needs to be done is difficult or uncomfortable. So we put off till tomorrow what should be done today.

The words of Psalm 34 remind us that the Lord solves problems for "people who do what is right" (v. 19 NCV) And usually, doing "what is right" means doing the uncomfortable work of confronting our problems sooner rather than later. So with no further ado, let the problem-solving begin . . . now.

Often, in the midst of great problems,
we stop short of the real blessing God has for us,
which is a fresh vision of who He is.

ANNE GRAHAM LOTZ

Faith does not eliminate problems.
Faith keeps you in a trusting relationship with
God in the midst of your problems.

HENRY BLACKABY

If you simply let a problem wash around in
your mind, it will seem greater and much more
vague than it will appear on close examination.

DOROTHEA BRANDE

A woman softens her own troubles
by generously solacing those of others.

FRANÇOISE D'AUBEGNE MAINTENON

MORE FROM GOD'S WORD

People who do what is right may have many problems,
but the Lord will solve them all.

PSALM 34:19 NCV

Be joyful because you have hope.
Be patient when trouble comes, and pray at all times.

ROMANS 12:12 NCV

TODAY, I WILL THINK ABOUT . . .

The benefit of tackling problems sooner
rather than later.

A PRAYER TO START MY DAY

Lord, sometimes my problems are simply too big for
me, but they are never too big for You. Let me turn
my troubles over to You, Lord, and let me trust in
You today and for all eternity. **Amen

SPIRITUAL GROWTH DAY BY DAY

BUT GROW IN THE GRACE AND KNOWLEDGE OF
OUR LORD AND SAVIOR JESUS CHRIST.
TO HIM BE THE GLORY, BOTH NOW AND
TO THE DAY OF ETERNITY.

2 PETER 3:18 NASB

The journey toward spiritual maturity lasts a lifetime. As Christians, we can and should continue to grow in the love and the knowledge of our Savior as long as we live. Norman Vincent Peale had the following advice for believers of all ages: "Ask the God who made you to keep remaking you." That advice, of course, is perfectly sound, but often ignored.

When we cease to grow, either emotionally or spiritually, we do ourselves a profound disservice. But, if we study God's Word, if we obey His commandments, and if we live in the center of His will, we will not be "stagnant" believers; we will, instead, be growing Christians . . . and that's exactly what God intends for us to be.

Life is a series of choices and decisions. Each day, we make countless decisions that can bring us closer to God . . . or not. When we live according to the principles contained in God's Holy Word, we embark upon a journey of spiritual maturity that results in life abundant and life eternal.

The search for grace, costly grace, involves
the acceptance of pain and the creative grief
which accompanies growth into maturity.

MADELEINE L'ENGLE

The disappointment has come, not because
God desires to hurt you or make you miserable or
to demoralize you, or ruin your life, or keep you
from ever knowing happiness. He wants you to be
perfect and complete in every aspect,
lacking nothing. It's not the easy times that
make you more like Jesus, but the hard times.

KAY ARTHUR

Real freedom means to welcome the responsibility it
brings, to welcome the God-control it requires,
to welcome the discipline that results,
to welcome the maturity it creates.

EUGENIA PRICE

MORE FROM GOD'S WORD

Therefore let us leave the elementary teachings about Christ and go on to maturity . . . .

HEBREWS 6:1 NIV

He who began a good work in you will carry it on to completion until the day of Christ Jesus.

PHILIPPIANS 1:6 NIV

TODAY, I WILL THINK ABOUT . . .

The importance of continuing to grow in the knowledge and love of the Lord.

A PRAYER TO START MY DAY

Thank You, Lord, that I am not yet what I am to become. The Holy Scripture tells me that You are at work in my life, continuing to help me grow and to mature in the faith. Show me Your wisdom, Father, and let me live according to Your Word and Your will. **Amen

WISDOM FOR TODAY

IF YOU NEED WISDOM—IF YOU WANT TO KNOW
WHAT GOD WANTS YOU TO DO—ASK HIM,
AND HE WILL GLADLY TELL YOU.
HE WILL NOT RESENT YOUR ASKING.

JAMES 1:5 NLT

Where will you find wisdom today? Will you seek it from God or from the world? As a thoughtful woman living in a society that is filled with temptations and distractions, you know that the world's brand of "wisdom" is everywhere . . . and it is dangerous. You live in a world where it's all too easy to stray far from the ultimate source of wisdom: God's Holy Word.

When you commit yourself to daily study of God's Word—and when you live according to His commandments—you will become wise . . . in time. But don't expect to open your Bible today and be wise tomorrow. Wisdom is not like a mushroom; it does not spring up overnight. It is, instead, like a majestic oak tree that starts as a tiny acorn, grows into a sapling, and eventually reaches up to the sky, tall and strong.

Today and every day, as a way of understanding God's plan for your life, you should study His Word and live by it. When you do, you will accumulate a storehouse of wisdom that will enrich your own life and the lives of your family members, your friends, and the world.

Knowledge can be learned, but wisdom
must be earned. Wisdom is knowledge . . . lived.

SHEILA WALSH

He teaches us, not just to let us see ourselves
correctly, but to help us see him correctly.

KATHY TROCCOLI

Our first step toward gaining God's wisdom is
to know what we do not know;
that is, to be aware of our shortcomings.

DIANNA BOOHER

Wisdom takes us beyond the realm of mere
right and wrong. Wisdom takes into account
our personalities, our strengths, our weaknesses,
and even our present state of mind.

CHARLES STANLEY

Don't expect wisdom to come into your life like
great chunks of rock on a conveyor belt.
Wisdom comes privately from God as a byproduct of
right decisions, godly reactions, and the application
of spiritual principles to daily circumstances.

CHARLES SWINDOLL

MORE FROM GOD'S WORD

Teach me Your way, O LORD;
I will walk in Your truth.

PSALM 86:11 NASB

The fear of the LORD is the beginning of wisdom,
and knowledge of the Holy One is understanding.

PROVERBS 9:10 NIV

TODAY, I WILL THINK ABOUT . . .

The difference between the world's "wisdom"
and God's true wisdom.

A PRAYER TO START MY DAY

Lord, make me a woman of wisdom and
discernment. I seek wisdom, Lord, not as the world
gives, but as You give. Lead me in Your ways and
teach me from Your Word so that, in time,
my wisdom might glorify Your kingdom
and Your Son. **Amen

TODAY: GOD'S GIFT TO YOU

THIS IS THE DAY THE LORD HAS MADE;
WE WILL REJOICE AND BE GLAD IN IT.

PSALM 118:24 NKJV

This day is a blessed gift from God. And as Christians, we have countless reasons to rejoice. Yet on some days, when the demands of life threaten to overwhelm us, we don't feel much like rejoicing. Instead of celebrating God's glorious creation, we may find ourselves frustrated by the obligations of today and worried by the uncertainties of tomorrow.

Every day should be a time for prayer and celebration as we consider the Good News of God's free gift: salvation through Jesus Christ. May we—as believers who have so much to celebrate—never fail to praise our Creator by rejoicing in His glorious handiwork.

The familiar words of Psalm 118:24 remind us that "This is the day the Lord has made," and we are instructed to make this day a time to rejoice. So, whatever this day holds for you, begin it and end it with God as your partner and Christ as your Savior. And throughout the day, give thanks to the One who created you and saved you. God's love for you is infinite. Accept it joyfully . . . and be thankful.

Submit each day to God, knowing that He
is God over all your tomorrows.

KAY ARTHUR

Love, joy, peace, patience, kindness, goodness,
faithfulness, gentleness, and self-control.
To these I commit my day. If I succeed, I will give
thanks. If I fail, I will seek his grace.
And then, when this day is done,
I will place my head on my pillow and rest.

MAX LUCADO

God gave you this glorious day.
Don't disappoint Him. Use it for His glory.

MARIE T. FREEMAN

Today is a gift from God.
That's why it is called "The Present."

ANONYMOUS

Each day, each moment is so pregnant
with eternity that if we "tune in" to it,
we can hardly contain the joy.

GLORIA GAITHER

MORE FROM GOD'S WORD

*While it is daytime, we must continue doing the work of
the One who sent me. Night is coming,
when no one can work.*

JOHN 9:4 NCV

TODAY, I WILL THINK ABOUT . . .

The importance of *living* in the present moment
and the importance of *celebrating*
the present moment.

A PRAYER TO START MY DAY

Lord, You have given me another day of life;
let me celebrate this day, and let me use it according
to Your plan. I praise You, Father, for my life and for
the friends and family members who make it rich.
Enable me to live each moment to the fullest
as I give thanks for Your creation, for Your love,
and for Your Son. **Amen

ACCEPTING GOD'S LOVE TODAY

FOR GOD LOVED THE WORLD IN THIS WAY:
HE GAVE HIS ONLY SON, SO THAT EVERYONE
WHO BELIEVES IN HIM WILL NOT PERISH
BUT HAVE ETERNAL LIFE.

JOHN 3:16 HCSB

St. Augustine observed, "God loves each of us as if there were only one of us." Do you believe those words? Do you seek to have an intimate, one-on-one relationship with your Heavenly Father, or are you satisfied to keep Him at a "safe" distance?

Sometimes, in the crush of our daily duties, God may seem far away, but He is not. God is everywhere we have ever been and everywhere we will ever go. He is with us night and day; He knows our thoughts and our prayers. And, when we earnestly seek Him, we will find Him because He is here, waiting patiently for us to reach out to Him.

Let us reach out to Him today and always. And let us praise Him for the glorious gifts that have transformed us today and forever. Amen.

Praise the Father for his loving kindness;
tenderly cares He for His erring children.
Praise Him.

ELIZABETH R. CHARLES

O love of God, how deep and great,
Far deeper than man's deepest hate.

CORRIE TEN BOOM

There is no secret that can separate you from
God's love; there is no secret that can separate you
from His blessings; there is no secret
that is worth keeping from His grace.

SERITA ANN JAKES

No part of our prayers creates a greater feeling of joy
than when we praise God for who He is. He is our
Master Creator, our Father, our source of all love.

SHIRLEY DOBSON

MORE FROM GOD'S WORD

If My people who are called by My name will humble themselves, and pray and seek My face, and turn from their wicked ways, then I will hear from heaven, and will forgive their sin and heal their land.

2 CHRONICLES 7:14 NKJV

TODAY, I WILL THINK ABOUT . . .

Christ's sacrifice for me . . . and God's love for me.

A PRAYER TO START MY DAY

Dear Lord, for the love You have shown me and the blessings You have given me, I thank You and I praise You. Your Son died so that I might receive the blessing of eternal love and eternal life. I will praise You today, tomorrow, and forever, Lord, for Your love, for Your mercy, and for Your Son. **Amen

BIBLE VERSES
TO
CONSIDER

HOLY SPIRIT

*The true children of God are those
who let God's Spirit lead them.*

ROMANS 8:14 NCV

*May the God of hope fill you with all joy and
peace as you trust in him, so that you may overflow
with hope by the power of the Holy Spirit.*

ROMANS 15:13 NIV

If we live in the Spirit, let us also walk in the Spirit.

GALATIANS 5:25 KJV

*And when the Holy Spirit comes on you,
you will be able to be my witnesses in Jerusalem,
all over Judea and Samaria,
even to the ends of the world.*

ACTS 1:8 MSG

I WILL PUT MY SPIRIT IN YOU
AND YOU WILL LIVE . . . .

EZEKIEL 37:14 NIV

GOD'S WILL

Morning by morning he wakens me and
opens my understanding to his will.
The Sovereign LORD has spoke to me,
and I have listened.

ISAIAH 50:4-5 NLT

And yet, LORD, you are our Father.
We are the clay, and you are the potter.
We are all formed by your hand.

ISAIAH 64:8 NLT

All that the Father giveth me shall come to me;
and him that cometh to me I will in no wise cast out.
For I came down from heaven, not to do mine own will,
but the will of him that sent me.

JOHN 6:37-38 KJV

. . . not my will, but thine, be done.

LUKE 22:42 KJV

FOR WHOEVER DOES THE WILL
OF GOD IS MY BROTHER AND
MY SISTER AND MOTHER.

MARK 3:35 NKJV

FRIENDS

*Greater love has no one than this,
that he lay down his life for his friends.*

JOHN 15:13 NIV

*A friend loves you all the time,
and a brother helps in time of trouble.*

PROVERBS 17:17 NCV

*How good and pleasant it is when
brothers live together in unity!*

PSALM 133:1 NIV

*So don't lose a minute in building on what
you've been given, complementing your basic faith with
good character, spiritual understanding, alert discipline,
passionate patience, reverent wonder, warm friendliness,
and generous love, each dimension fitting into and
developing the others.*

2 PETER 1:5-7 MSG

As iron sharpens iron,
a friend sharpens a friend.

PROVERBS 27:17 NLT

HEALTH

Therefore, whether you eat or drink,
or whatever you do, do all to the glory of God.

1 CORINTHIANS 10:31 NKJV

Beloved, I pray that in all respects you may prosper and
be in good health, just as your soul prospers.

3 JOHN 1:2 NASB

Jesus Christ maketh thee whole.

ACTS 9:34 KJV

The LORD will take away from thee all sickness.

DEUTERONOMY 7:15 KJV

The power of the Lord was present to heal them.

LUKE 5:17 KJV

GOLDEN RULE

Each of you should look not only to your own interests,
but also to the interest of others.

PHILIPPIANS 2:4 NIV

Therefore, whatever you want men to do to you,
do also to them, for this is the Law and the Prophets.

MATTHEW 7:12 NKJV

Do to others as you would have them do to you.

LUKE 6:31 NIV

Yes indeed, it is good when you truly obey
our Lord's royal command found in the Scriptures:
"Love your neighbor as yourself."

JAMES 2:8 NLT

See that no one pays back evil for evil,
but always try to do good to each other
and to everyone else.

1 THESSALONIANS 5:15 NLT

MATERIALISM

For the love of money is a root of all kinds of evil,
for which some have strayed from the faith
in their greediness, and pierced themselves through
with many sorrows.

1 TIMOTHY 6:10 NKJV

Then Jesus said to them, "Be careful and guard
against all kinds of greed. Life is not measured by
how much one owns."

LUKE 12:15 NCV

Do not store up for yourselves treasures on earth,
where moth and rust destroy, and where thieves break
in and steal. But store up for yourselves treasures in
heaven, where moth and rust do not destroy,
and where thieves do not break in and steal.
For where your treasure is, there your heart will be also.

MATTHEW 6:19-21 NIV

Such is the end of all who go after ill-gotten gain;
it takes away the lives of those who get it.

PROVERBS 1:19 NIV

WHOEVER LOVES MONEY
NEVER HAS MONEY ENOUGH;
WHOEVER LOVES WEALTH IS NEVER
SATISFIED WITH HIS INCOME.

ECCLESIASTES 5:10 NIV

GOD'S PROVISION

*And God will generously provide all you need.
Then you will always have everything you need and
plenty left over to share with others.*

2 CORINTHIANS 9:8 NLT

*Steep your life in God-reality, God-initiative,
God-provisions. Don't worry about missing out.
You'll find all your everyday human concerns
will be met.*

MATTHEW 6:33 MSG

*I will lift up my eyes to the mountains;
from whence shall my help come? My help comes
from the LORD, who made the heaven and earth.*

PSALM 121:1-2 NASB

*I'll lead them into lush pasture so they can roam
the mountain pastures of Israel, graze at leisure,
feed in the rich pastures on the mountains of Israel.*

EZEKIEL 34:14 MSG

AND MY GOD SHALL SUPPLY
ALL YOUR NEED ACCORDING
TO HIS RICHES IN GLORY
BY CHRIST JESUS.

PHILIPPIANS 4:19 NKJV

GRACE

*For it is by grace you have been saved, through faith—
and this not from yourselves, it is the gift of God—
not by works, so that no one can boast.*

EPHESIANS 2:8-9 NIV

*Therefore let us draw near with confidence
to the throne of grace, so that we may receive mercy and
find grace to help in time of need.*

HEBREWS 4:16 NASB

*For if, by the trespass of the one man, death reigned
through that one man, how much more will those
who receive God's abundant provision of grace and of
the gift of righteousness reign in life through
the one man, Jesus Christ.*

ROMANS 5:17 NIV

*You then, my son, be strong in the grace
that is in Christ Jesus.*

2 TIMOTHY 2:1 NIV

BUT GOD GIVES US EVEN MORE
GRACE, AS THE SCRIPTURE SAYS,
"GOD IS AGAINST THE PROUD,
BUT HE GIVES GRACE
TO THE HUMBLE."

JAMES 4:6 NCV

HEAVEN

*Let not your heart be troubled: ye believe in God,
believe also in me. In my Father's house are many
mansions: if it were not so, I would have told you.
I go to prepare a place for you. And if I go and prepare
a place for you, I will come again, and receive you unto
myself; that where I am, there ye may be also.*

JOHN 14:1-3 KJV

*Your kingdom is an everlasting kingdom,
and Your dominion endures throughout all generations.*

PSALM 145:13 NASB

*As you go, preach this message:
"The kingdom of heaven is near."*

MATTHEW 10:7 NIV

*For we know that, if our earthly house of this tabernacle
were dissolved, we have a building of God,
a house not made with hands, eternal in the heavens.*

2 CORINTHIANS 5:1 KJV

For our citizenship is in heaven,
from which also we eagerly
wait for a Savior,
the Lord Jesus Christ.

Philippians 3:20 nasb

GOODNESS

The LORD approves of those who are good,
but he condemns those who plan wickedness.

PROVERBS 12:2 NLT

A good man out of the good treasure of his heart brings
forth good things, and an evil man out of
the evil treasure brings forth evil things.

MATTHEW 12:35 NKJV

See that no one renders evil for evil to anyone,
but always pursue what is good both
for yourselves and for all.

1 THESSALONIANS 5:15 NKJV

For we are His workmanship, created in Christ Jesus for
good works, which God prepared beforehand
that we should walk in them.

EPHESIANS 2:10 NKJV

ABHOR THAT WHICH IS EVIL;
CLEAVE TO THAT WHICH IS GOOD.

ROMANS 12:9 KJV

GOD'S TIMING

Humble yourselves, therefore,
under God's mighty hand,
that he may lift you up in due time.

1 PETER 5:6 NIV

He [Jesus] said to them:
"It is not for you to know the times or
dates the Father has set by his own authority."

ACTS 1:7 NIV

To everything there is a season,
a time for every purpose under heaven.

ECCLESIASTES 3:1 NKJV

This is what the LORD says:
"In the time of my favor I will answer you,
and in the day of salvation I will help you . . . .

ISAIAH 49:8 NIV

I WAIT FOR THE LORD,
MY SOUL WAITS, AND IN HIS WORD
I PUT MY HOPE.

PSALM 130:5 NIV

THE BIBLE

*There's nothing like the written Word of God for
showing you the way to salvation through faith in Christ
Jesus. Every part of Scripture is God-breathed and
useful one way or another, showing us truth,
exposing our rebellion, correcting our mistakes,
training us to live God's way. Through the Word
we are put together and shaped up for
the tasks God has for us.*

2 TIMOTHY 3:15-17 MSG

*Man shall not live by bread alone,
but by every word that proceeds from the mouth of God.*

MATTHEW 4:4 NKJV

*You will be a good servant of Christ Jesus,
constantly nourished on the words of the faith and
of the sound doctrine which you have been following.*

1 TIMOTHY 4:6 NASB

*Every word of God is flawless;
he is a shield to those who take refuge in him.*

PROVERBS 30:5 NIV

FOR I AM NOT ASHAMED OF
THE GOSPEL, BECAUSE IT IS
GOD'S POWER FOR SALVATION
TO EVERYONE WHO BELIEVES.

ROMANS 1:16 HCSB

GENTLENESS

Be peaceable, gentle, showing every consideration
for all men.

TITUS 3:2 NASB

Let your gentleness be evident to all.
The Lord is near.

PHILIPPIANS 4:5 NIV

Are there those among you who are truly wise and
understanding? Then they should show it by living right
and doing good things with a gentleness
that comes from wisdom.

JAMES 3:13 NCV

So, as those who have been chosen of God,
holy and beloved, put on a heart of compassion,
kindness, humility, gentleness and patience.

COLOSSIANS 3:12 NASB

ALWAYS BE HUMBLE, GENTLE,
AND PATIENT, ACCEPTING
EACH OTHER IN LOVE.

EPHESIANS 4:2 NCV

FOLLOWING CHRIST

Whoever serves me must follow me.
Then my servant will be with me everywhere I am.
My Father will honor anyone who serves me.

JOHN 12:26 NCV

Follow Me, He told them, "and I will make you
fishers of men!" Immediately they left their nets and
followed Him.

MATTHEW 4:19-20 HCSB

No one can serve two masters.
Either he will hate the one and love the other,
or he will be devoted to the one and despise the other.

MATTHEW 6:24

Then he told them what they could expect
for themselves: "Anyone who intends to come
with me has to let me lead."

LUKE 9:23 MSG

AND WHEN HE HAD SPOKEN THIS,
HE SAID TO HIM,
"FOLLOW ME."

JOHN 21:19 NKJV

GOD'S PROMISES

For you have need of endurance,
so that when you have done the will of God,
you may receive what was promised.

HEBREWS 10:36 NASB

As for God, his way is perfect.
All the LORD's promises prove true.
He is a shield for all who look to him for protection.

PSALM 18:30 NLT

And we desire that each one of you show the same
diligence so as to realize the full assurance of hope
until the end, so that you will not be sluggish,
but imitators of those who through faith and
patience inherit the promises.

HEBREWS 6:11-12 NASB

LORD, sustain me as you promised, that I may live!
Do not let my hope be crushed.

PSALM 119:116 NLT

LET US HOLD FAST THE CONFESSION
OF OUR HOPE WITHOUT WAVERING,
FOR HE WHO PROMISED
IS FAITHFUL.

HEBREWS 10:23 NASB